BUILD MY KINGDOM THROUGH
YOUR BARRENNESS AND I WILL
BLESS YOU

BUILD MY KINGDOM THROUGH YOUR BARRENNESS AND I WILL BLESS YOU

PORSHEA WILKINS

CONTENTS

To my beloved husband, provider, protector and love of my life Nnamdi Jarrod Wilkins-Agomo. It is my greatest honor to be your wife, best friend and partner in life. In sickness and health, for richer and for poorer, til death do us part I am yours.

To my handsome loving boys Aiden Nkwachi Wilkins-Agomo and Nathan Akachi Wilkins-Agomo. You've changed my life forever. Being your mother is my greatest joy. I love you to infinity and beyond and then some more.

To my parents Leslie and Anthony - thank you for your endless support, laughter and love. I'm blessed to be your daughter.

To my heavenly Father. You reign above it all. Thank you isn't enough. I pray my work and life make you proud.

Introduction

Long story short as to how we got here. After getting married in 2014 the Lord took me on a 5-year prophetic, cross-continental journey through infertility to conceive our son Aiden. I had a myomectomy performed to remove eight grapefruit sized fibroids. During my recovery the Lord called me into ministry by telling me *"My daughters are hungry"*. With no formal theology training or official service in any church. His instructions were simple, *"**Read my word and tell them what I tell you.**"* So, I packed up my bible and my nerves and did what the Lord told me to do. I taught my first sermon on a conference call line on January 5, 2015. I called it Straight Talk Woman Talk because we needed to hear real testimonies that are unfiltered and authentic. We'd meet every Monday, and I'd share what the Lord gave me and invite guests to share their testimony. The Lord would give me women's name and faces in my sleep or in a vision that He wanted to share their testimonies. Women I didn't know at all or know well. I'd google or search for them on social media then message them what the Lord told me. They'd join me for a session and the result would always confirm it was the Lord's doing.

The weekly conference call led to an in-person event in 2016 called the Straight Talk Woman Talk Intensive. My husband and I are entrepreneurs and our business had a lot of expenses so there wasn't much left over for something like this. The hotel I chose was out of my budget, yet as I began to work, the Lord provided. I still get testimonies about it to this day. I then began to host small group meetings at hotels called Straight Talk Woman Talk Impart Sessions in Texas and Georgia. Again, no budget to do it, yet as I began to work, the Lord provided.

In 2018 while on a business trip to South Africa, I was sitting in church with my Husband and our friend when the Lord said again *"My daughters are hungry"*. I was extremely reluctant because I knew what that meant. How was I going to do a Straight Talk Woman Talk Intensive on another continent, in 90 days, with people I only knew through business? Who would come? How will I pay for it? How will I plan it? Where would it be? Again, as I began to work, the Lord provided.

During all of these events – I was still without child. I'd pray for women, witness them get healed, pregnant and deliver their promised babies. All while barren myself. I felt like a hypocrite. I questioned my call. I told God I didn't want to do it anymore. I even quit a few times vowing to never do it again. Then God would send a prophetic word, song, or encounter that would light my fire again, and I'd dig up whatever faith I had in my tank and do what He said. He told me *"If you build My Kingdom through your barrenness, I will bless you."* I believed Him so I built.

I go into great detail about my Supernatural Pregnancy journey in my book *You're Not Infertile. You're Just Not in Timing.* My testimony involves, warfare at the ocean, demonic attacks, dreams of tornadoes, a botched IVF attempt, miracle fibroid removal and more, and after five years of building through my barrenness as the Lord told me, I gave birth to our son Aiden Nkwachi Wilkins-Agomo on July 30, 2020 my 39th birthday. A gift so perfect only God could give it. His middle name Nkwachi, is Igbo (Nigerian) and means "God's Promise".

After his birth I got back out to build by sharing my testimony with others. The events that unfolded next were nothing short of supernatural.

CHAPTER 1

The Build

S uddenly everything I encountered along the journey began to make more sense. I was invigorated and had to release the refined fire shut up in my bones, so I wrote my first book mentioned above and filmed a mini-Docuseries with my Supernatural Pregnancy testimony. Then the Lord told me again *"My daughters are hungry"* so in March 2022 I hosted the first Supernatural Pregnancy Summit. It was powerful. The Lord told me to create prayer petition forms for attendees to fill out and lay at the altar during our time together. He also told me at 3:33pm we are to do as His word says in *Jeremiah 33:3 'Call to Me, and I will answer you, and show you great and mighty things, which you do not know.'* We are to stop whatever we're doing in that moment, go to the altar with all the prayer petitions and call upon the Lord with prayer, praise and worship, as if our life depends on it – because it does.

I had a crew of Purpose Midwives some who also had supernatural pregnancies and some who had powerful supernatural testimonies. One woman shared how she had to rush her healthy teenage son to the hospital who randomly felt sick. When they arrived, she discovered his organs looked like a bomb had gone off inside his body. He was sepsis and septic, needing new lungs and a new heart, literally walking into deaths door, but thank God he had a mother who knew how to fight. She assembled a prayer coalition, and for 24 hours a day they prayed for him asking the Lord to make it like it never happened. She visited him daily and stood on the report of the Lord. What happened after a few days

1

was nothing short of a miracle, he got up and walked out of the hospital as if nothing ever happened. The entire hospital was in shock and wanted to do a study to not only show what happened medically, but how the supernatural hand of God supersedes natural medicine. Her testimony was featured on television and newspapers. I highly recommend her book *Like It Never Happened* by Pastor Nadine Smith.

The testimonies that flowed out of the Supernatural Pregnancy Summit were all confirmation that the Lord was there. Miracle healing, marriages, businesses and babies. One woman, who was my hair stylist at the time, was a single mother of two children petitioning for a husband. About two months later not only did she meet a great guy and get married, they also had a son together! Another Midwife, who is my best friend, and a few years older than me in her late 40's shared her testimony there as well. Like me, she also had fibroids, but she didn't discover hers until she miscarried. Tragically she had to vaginally deliver the baby still born. I remember her sharing that after inducing her, the nurses were telling her to push and push, but nothing was happening. She had to yell back at them *"I don't know how!"* That's when they realized it was her first experience giving birth. It was devastating. After that she had to have a myomectomy to remove the fibroids. Despite the setback and trauma she continued to believe and after a few more miscarriages and rounds of IVF the Lord healed her womb and blessed she and her husband with a son. She was scheduled for a c-section, but he came vaginally with only two pushes. The Lord replaced the ashes of her first vaginal birth experience and gave her beauty for it with an effortless one. She and her husband wanted more and since then the Lord has blessed them with another son, also through IVF, but this time a c-section was best for she and baby. She jokes now that she went through all of that just for both boys to look nothing like her. Her husband literally copied and pasted them both!

Another one of the Midwives, Pastor Shannon Hinton wasn't believing for more children of her own, as hers are adults and she's a grandmother, but she was supernaturally pregnant with a promise for a building for their church. She put it on her petition and a few weeks after the Supernatural Pregnancy Summit, after years of being denied approval with no explanation, suddenly every no became a yes and they were able to purchase their church building! Her book *Sleeping Giant Come Forth* is a faith activating read, I highly recommend.

During this time, I wasn't believing for more children of my own, I was believing for children for those who were battling infertility like I was before. I wanted to be for others what I didn't have for myself. It doesn't just take a village to raise a child, it takes a village to create one as well. So, I started to build that village creating a group called Supernatural Mamas and began hosting village sessions via zoom monthly. The ladies share where they are in their fertility journey, we laugh, cry, listen, learn, love and pray. A Kingdom community that understands life doesn't stop because you desire to have a child. We still have to be wives, friends, employees, employers, daughters, sisters, cousins, consultants and more. You need people who can help you wade those waters without judgment and that's what we do.

CHAPTER 2

Pink Fetus

In August 2023 after a 21-day water only fast with my home church, the Lord told me to have another Supernatural Pregnancy Summit, but this time take it on tour across Texas. Although I was born and raised in Texas I didn't know people in every city, then the Holy Spirit reminded me I didn't know anyone in South Africa in 2018 either yet He provided! So, I began to work. This time He was clear the Supernatural Pregnancy Summit was to be hosted in churches versus hotels. Hotels are easy to book, churches require relationships which I didn't have outside of Houston where I lived. He told me to have one in Houston in September, Dallas in October, San Antonio in November and El Paso in December, but it wasn't until I executed one that He would release the location for the next one so everything was back-to-back and sometimes to the wire to execute. A true faith walk.

Finding a church in Houston was easy since I have many friends in ministry here. During my 21 days of fasting, I had 21 prayer petitions, one was for the Lord to show us His glory. I wanted to have a bold visual encounter like I've heard others share and read about in the Bible. On September 8th the night before the Supernatural Pregnancy Summit, He answered. As we were testing the live stream, I looked on the computer screen and couldn't believe my eyes. The altar was covered in a white glare and right above it was a pink figure shaped like a 6-week-old baby in the womb.

**Pink fetus and the Glory of the Lord -
September 8, 2023**

A pink fetus resting on the glory of the Lord sitting there for us to witness. I went live on my social media just so everyone could witness. It was the same church Pastor Shannon petitioned for a year prior at the first Supernatural Pregnancy Summit, she and her son were able to witness it with me, they were also blown away. There was nothing pink in the room, no special lighting or decor, yet there it was clear as day the Lord saying *"Daughter, your daughter is ready. My daughters are coming."* I took that literal as in women will give birth to daughters and spiritual as in His daughters are arising to build.

The next day, September 9, 2023 the church was soaked in His glory. You could feel it the moment you walked in the door. When the clock struck 3:33p something happened that can only be described as miraculous. The atmosphere shifted. I grabbed the gold vase full of prayer petitions and poured three bottles of anointing oil over them as we prayed. My hands felt electric. There were sharp currents running through my fingers. The feeling is similar to when you hit your funny bone – lots of tingling and fire. After what we witnessed the night before I knew the

Father was doing something major for us all. The picture of me holding the vase in the air that I use for marketing is the embodiment of that moment. My other favorite photo is of Aiden in his cute little outfit, holding a microphone and making his way to the pulpit. He is a pure worshiper and orator. If there is a microphone, in any room, in any building - he wants it, just so he can praise the Lord. Having him with me while I share our testimony is a dream come true and testament of the word becoming flesh. The Lord is a keeper of His promises – yes and Amen!

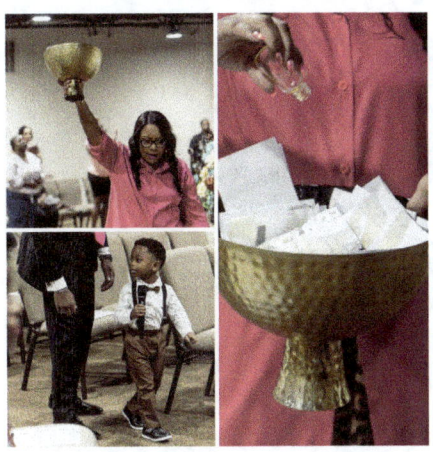

**Supernatural Pregnancy Summit -
September 9, 2023**

A few days later I was in my office unpacking everything from the event, getting ready for my prayer time, when the Holy Spirit told me to get the prayer petitions and lay them out while I prayed. They were all soaked in the anointing oil so I figured they'd have ink all over them from the pens people used to write with. What happened next brought me to my knees. As I pulled out each sheet of oil-soaked paper the words written were not only readable some of the words were bold! Electricity ran through my body and I wept in pure awe and adoration for the Father. He told me to read each one, and as I did, He showed me snapshots of the person who wrote it. I could see them working, crying, driving, laughing, sitting, doctor appointments, walking and praying, all of them weighed down with a deep yearning for what they'd petitioned for. I remember that feeling because not too long ago that was me. All I could do was cry out to the Lord praying in tongues. I don't know how long I was in the spirit but my knees were hurting afterwards for being on them for so long. I laid down on my office floor until my body re-calibrated. It was powerful.

CHAPTER 3

Touring by Faith

After Houston, I asked the Lord where to go in October. He said Dallas. Every event I did always had other ministers – Midwives – all operating within the five-fold gifts written in Ephesians 4:11-12 - pastor, prophet, teacher, evangelist and apostle. I began promoting without a church to host it in, knowing God will provide. I had relationships with people in Dallas who had relationships with churches so finding a location for that was pretty easy. Getting it solidified was a challenge that ran up to the last minute, but overall things went perfect. The power of the Holy Spirit hit the room like a wave and the fire of God was released. If you go to my website SupernaturalPregnancy.com you'll see the replays. You'll also see Aiden with his microphone prophesying and preaching right along with everyone at three years old! He has a strong apostolic anointing on his life just like his Daddy. I got home, unpacked the anointing oil-soaked prayer petitions again to lay out during my prayer time wondering if they'd be readable and I'd have the same experience. They were and I did. Hallelujah!

Next up was San Antonio, I had one connection there, but they didn't have any relationships with churches. I was on Instagram one day and the Holy Spirit told me to reach out to a woman in ministry I recently connected with. She lived in Dallas, so I didn't know how she could help with San Antonio, but the Holy Spirit told me to contact her so I did. I asked if she knew anyone in San Antonio with a church. To which she said her uncle has a church and he lets her use his all the time and would let me too if she asked. Winning! I shared it online and about fifteen people came! I'm always excited when people show up. I know at least one will and that's enough, my audience is the Lord anyway. I lean on Him so He sends women and men fighting the same fight I had to fight. The fertility challenges they are facing are mind blowing. Things I never heard of before, some I have, all requiring miracles. Partial hysterectomy's, endometriosis, blocked fallopian tubes, miscarriages, past abortions, no sperm, no eggs, fibroids inside and outside the uterus, sickle cell, birth defects, abnormal menstrual cycles with excessive bleeding, ectopic pregnancies the list goes on. Every single woman and couple holding onto a promise from the Lord that they will have a child. Many single, not only believing for healing, but for a spouse too! Feeling like damaged goods, wondering if they'd be able to marry once they share their condition with someone they are dating. The mental and emotional weight is heavy on the heart. But God. One of the ladies the Lord said to prophesy *"prepare your wedding registry"*. She confirmed she was believing for healing in her womb and a spouse. She left and immediately took action preparing her registry by faith. Five months later she got engaged! When I got home, I once again unpacked the anointing oil-soaked prayer petitions to lay out during my prayer time wondering if they'd be readable and I'd have the same experience. They were and I did. Hallelujah!

After the San Antonio Supernatural Pregnancy Summit, the Lord isolated me. He told me *"Just you from now on"*, no other Midwives. I was concerned I wouldn't have enough to say to fill in our three hours together, but I was wrong. I realized I was the one who carried exactly what the people He was sending needed. I want to always be in alignment with His will, and that meant yielding to the Holy Spirit. Whatever that looked like was fine with me as long as it would be considered obedient to Him. In Luke chapter 13 there was a woman who was bent over from demonic possession for eighteen years. Jesus saw and healed her. There was a man who saw Jesus perform this miracle and began to chastise Him for it because it was the sabbath and no one is supposed to work on the sabbath. Jesus called the man a hypocrite because he still feeds his animals on the sabbath, and if the animals can get relief, then this woman who was tortured for eighteen years can as well. When I read that I heard the Lord say *"release control"*. Sometimes we can be so rigid, bent over and structured in an attempt to maintain control that we leave no room for the Holy Spirit – our Helper – to help! He wants to flow through you, but you're fixed! God wants to interrupt your flow and break protocol for you, but you have to release control so that He can. When you step back, miracles step in.

I recognized that moment, and to make sure I didn't miss my miracle He sent me to a place where He knew I wouldn't know anyone and that no other Midwife would be able to travel to - El Paso, Texas. I'd never even set foot on that side of Texas in my then 42 years of life. I knew absolutely no one who would even know anyone, nevertheless I booked our flights and hotel and began promoting without a church to host it in, trusting God to provide.

To find one I did what I did back in the beginning of my journey in 2015 when He'd show me women's names and faces to invite to the Straight Talk Woman Talk Monday conference calls – I googled churches to call! I'd say to whoever answered:

Hello! My name is Porshea Wilkins, I live in Houston, Texas and I'm wondering if you could help me. I'm looking for a place to host my Supernatural Pregnancy Summit. The Lord took me on a 5-year prophetic cross-continental journey through infertility to give birth to my son on my 39th *birthday. Now that He blessed me, He told me to be a blessing to others and host events to share my testimony and activate their faith to believe for their babies and more. He said come to your city and since I don't know anyone there, I searched online, found you and wanted to see if your church was available to host or if you could connect me to one that may be.*

Most were gracious when saying no and gave a referral, some hung up on me when they heard Supernatural Pregnancy. I was tickled and I kept smiling and dialing knowing since the Lord was sending me, He will provide!

One day, as I'm googling churches in El Paso, I came across a directory that looked like the Yellow Pages. That's what we had back in the day – 90's and earlier – to find a phone number or address. There was a listing for a church so I went to their website and called the number. No one answered so I left a message, and as I was getting ready to exit the directory, I saw a different phone number from what was on the website, and I called.

A man answered, *Hello?* He didn't say anything about the church so I figured it was a cell phone.

I said *"Is this Shiloh Baptist Church?"*

He said *"Yes this is Reverend White"*.

I asked *"Are you the Pastor?"*

He said *"Yes I am!"*

I said *"oh wow! Ok awesome!"* Then gave him my elevator pitch.

He said, *"It sounds interesting, and I'd like to hear more, but I'm at the airport and my flight is boarding. Email me your information."*

I got his email and hung up the phone. The call was four minutes long and the most progress I'd gotten so I knew it was my yes. Considering Thanksgiving was coming up and the Supernatural Pregnancy Summit was only two weeks away I needed this to be it!

I sent him the info; we worked out all the details, and on December 8th my Husband, Aiden and I flew out in expectation for the Lord to move the next day. The church was an older one and a staple in the community. Beautiful building. They were finishing up practice for a Christmas program. They helped with music for praise and worship, a 14-year-old sang while her uncle played on keys and a young man on drums. No bells and whistles, but all glory. There were about fifteen people there. I shared my testimony, prophesied to a mother to be who desired twins, as well as a few others, including the Pastor. Their spirit bared witness and our hearts were full. Thinking I was done since the Lord hadn't given me any instruction for January, I was ready to pack up and go home to relax for the new year. I was exhausted. Traveling, planning, delivering the word, prophesying, leading, packing all the Supernatural Pregnancy Faith kits with pregnancy tests, anointing oil and communion cups etc… all with a three-year-old son and husband who still needed a present mother and wife, was a lot. After we were done, a mother and daughter approached me. I saw them when they walked in and knew they were special. I asked if they were from El Paso and they said no. They were from Monroe, Louisiana. I was taken back and asked *"You flew here?!"* they said yes. Then the daughter began to share that she found out about me from a friend of hers who sent her the live-stream for the Dallas Supernatural Pregnancy Summit. After watching she ordered my book, *You're Not Infertile. You're Just Not in Timing* and said she had to make it out to my next summit. Soon as I shared online about El Paso, she said they booked their flights.

I was so shocked and excited all at the same time! She's a successful attorney and her husband a well-known photographer and they'd been battling infertility for eight years. She and her husband decided to wait until they were married awhile before starting a family. Thinking it would be simple, only to discover it wasn't. At the time they'd already gone through multiple rounds of IVF (Invitro-fertilization) and at $10,000 - $20,000 each with no help from insurance, they were tapped out financially and needed a miracle. She and her mother shared they have a church in Monroe where her father is the Pastor and wanted to invite me and my family to come do a Supernatural Pregnancy Summit there. I immediately said yes!

CHAPTER 4

Supernatural Pregnancy Wonder

It was scheduled for January 27, 2024, I was exhausted but not surprised considering all that had been going on. Three days before our travel to Monroe, on January 24th I was sitting on the couch about to take a nap while my Husband was upstairs giving Aiden his bath and I heard the Holy Spirit say ***"Take a pregnancy test"***. I frowned and said *"What? For what?"* We weren't even thinking of having another baby, just enjoying the benefits of marriage. Then I remembered the pink fetus in September and thought *"Really Jesus?!"*. So, I get a pregnancy test from one of the Supernatural Pregnancy Faith Kits, go to the restroom and the moment I started peeing on the stick it instantly said PREGNANT. I was completely shocked! *Like how? Jesus, I asked you to give THEM a baby not us! We have our promise! What is this?!* Part of it was superficial for me too. I lost fifty pounds and was only twenty pounds away from my goal! My new wardrobe had to go to the back of my closet for the time being which I wasn't thrilled about.

I go upstairs and tell my husband I figured out why I'd been so tired. He was in denial to say the least. Took him a minute to grasp it, me too. We just got Aiden potty trained! He told me to drink some water and take another test to confirm. I did and it gave the same result – I was pregnant pregnant! Since we saw the pink fetus in September, we knew we were having a girl, so we named her and began talking to and about her just as we did with Aiden. Even told him he's having a baby sister.

He wasn't excited. His little emotions were all over the place initially. Three days later we packed up and flew to Monroe, Louisiana.

This time it felt different for me knowing I was pregnant; they took really excellent care of us, treating us like family and did a lot of the details so I wouldn't have to. I was able to focus on executing the assignment and making God proud. So many couples traveled to be there. It was such a powerful move of God. I saw so much of myself in their eyes. Many of the husbands looked helpless and drained. Its tough for them because they are providers and protectors and couldn't provide a solution or protect their wife from the pain. Some of them were the infertile ones – that's something men don't talk about. One of the ladies in my Supernatural Mamas group shared that for years they'd been trying to get pregnant but couldn't because her husband's sperm count was very low. They went back and forth to the doctor running tests trying to figure out why and was told his semen was toxic. The doctor prescribed her some medicine in the beginning that was supposed to help. They felt uneasy as time went by without any changes and decided to get a second opinion. We petitioned to the Lord for Him to reveal what the hidden issue was. A couple of days later, they visit the new doctor who was able to identify the problem which wasn't what she was taking the medicine for! In fact, it was the medicine the previous doctor prescribed that was making his semen toxic! Now they are checking to see if there is anything that can be done legally to get the thousands of dollars, they spent with the other doctor back. Through it all they were so grateful to finally know what the issue was so they can target it correctly and identify what they are going to do next. Infertility is big money so unfortunately there is a lot of corruption. Doctors will have you going down a path that isn't even necessary for your issues just so they can get more money. It's sad.

When I got home, and finally unpacked the anointing oil-soaked prayer petitions to lay out during my prayer time, I had the exact same experience as all the Supernatural Pregnancy Summit's before. Perfectly preserved paper, bold words and the fire of the Lord. God is so faithful!

CHAPTER 5

Supernatural Twins

Now that those assignments were complete, the Lord told me to rest so I could carry my pregnancy with peace. I couldn't reach my doctor who delivered Aiden so I had to find another – good old google again! We went to our first appointment on February 6th expecting to see a little tiny chicken nugget on the ultrasound and instead we saw a whole baby. Head, heart, lungs, ribs, bladder, legs, feet, arms, hands everything! The doctor asked *"when was your last period?"* I told her I don't remember. She said *"because you're measuring at about 11 weeks"*. My husband and I both yelled *WHATTT?!* Wild. I was literally going into my second trimester and had absolutely no idea I was pregnant. That means while I was on assignment, ministering in different cities – I was pregnant.

Let that sink in. I'm traveling with my miracle son, ministering to women and couples who need a miracle for children at the Supernatural Pregnancy Summit while Supernaturally pregnant! Listen! YOU CAN'T MAKE THIS UP! But God didn't stop there. While we're talking to our daughter in my belly, narrowing down names and preparing the baby registry we get the results for the genetic test which tells you the baby's gender. Our doctor says *"The chromosomes are XY. It's a boy"* to which I my super deep prophetic self said *"Well that's wrong because the Lord sent us a pink fetus in September."* He said *"Daughter, your daughter is ready"*. She laughed and said *"Well someone is having a girl, just not you right now!"* We laughed.

After getting the genetic results, I googled and saw that blood tests can say one thing while the baby is another, so it was possible the test was wrong. I told my husband it's a girl until we see different on the ultra-sound.

On April 16, 2024 we get to the 21-week anatomy scan ultra-sound and without hesitation our baby made sure we knew he was indeed a boy! Legs and little boy part straight up! *Here I am mommy!* Whelp! There he is! All I could think of was the pink fetus, wondering why would the Lord show me that but give us a son. After that appointment we all got in the car and while it was warming up, I opened up Facebook on my phone and the first post I saw was from Prophet Tomi Arayomi, he's the Pastor of the church I attend and did the 21-day fast with. His post was an encouraging and correcting one for the prophetic. He said getting a prophecy wrong doesn't mean you're a false prophet, it just means you're not God. It hit me. I read it out loud to my husband because he was also perplexed.

1 Corinthians 13:9-10 NKJV - For we know in part and we prophesy in part. But when that which is perfect has come, then that which is in part will be done away.

Years before we met, he received a prophecy that he'd have two daughters and one son, and his son would completely change his life, but instead he now has two sons and one daughter. We received so many prophecies and confirmations about Aiden, we knew for sure he was coming, and since the pink fetus was sent directly and visibly by the Father, we were even more sure we were having a girl this time. We laughed and said to each other, God just put us in check! He can do what He wants, when and how so simmer down, deflate your chest, adjust your ego and stay low under Him. I compared our new baby boy's ultrasound picture to the one I had of Aiden and was blown away when I saw the EXACT SAME DATE April 16, 2020 for both! That means

they were both conceived in November on the same date! Supernatural
Twins! Only God can do that!

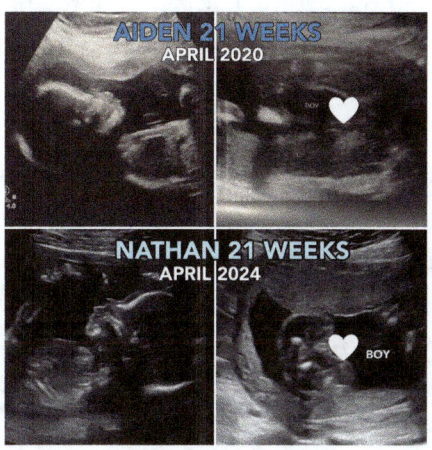

Supernatural Twins

My pregnancy was amazing. I prayed for a stress free and pain free
pregnancy and delivery, and based on my first experience with a tough
postpartum I made sure to pray for peace with that as well. Aiden's excitement grew as the days went by, we read tons of big brother books
and he attended all appointments with me, even when my husband had
to travel and miss them. He'd watch everything the doctor would do
and duplicate it when we got home, using his cars, dinosaurs, excava-
tors, random stuff, including my kitchen utensils he wasn't supposed to
play with, but did anyway, all as medical instruments. I had a million appointments at home and according to Dr. Aiden was a really good pa-
tient. I let him have his way so once his baby brother arrived, he'd adjust
well to sharing Mommy's time. He is a super mama's boy. My birthday
twin, so sharing me was not caring for him!

I didn't get to have a baby shower with Aiden because the world was
shut down in 2020 from the pandemic so I was excited to have one with
Nathan. I love the creative process and I'm always saving decor, DIY

and event inspiration I like on Instagram. While searching for kid birthday party ideas I'd also come across baby shower decor. My favorite was Winnie the Pooh and since we've been really blessed in our businesses, I knew I'd have a good budget for all the bells and whistles I wanted, but as I began to plan it, I got some resistance from my Husband I couldn't understand why. All he would say was it's handled you don't need to do anything. While that sounded good, it wasn't because whoever was doing the handling didn't know what I wanted and I since this is my first and probably last baby shower, I wanted what I'd been picturing for years and couldn't have with Aiden. This was a very big deal for me. A couple of days went by and the more I thought about it the sadder I'd get. I'd tell myself to be grateful for whatever it was, but then remember all the work I'd done and sacrificed not just for my ministry but of body – a myomectomy, c-section and another c-section planned – that's three times on the operating table. Three times being cut open and sewed shut. I am the ministry! I have become a living sacrifice for all that I preach and teach. I deserve my Winnie the Pooh! I couldn't take sitting back and letting someone else execute their vision versus the one God put in my heart, so one morning after sobbing I sent a text message to my friend Pastor Shannon, I spoke of earlier in my testimony. She called me on Face-time and told me it was her fault my husband was acting that way. What I didn't know is she called him many months prior to tell him that she wanted to surprise me for my baby shower, so he told my mom and they began working on it with some of the other Midwives. I cried again, but tears of joy. She sent me some of the ideas the planner had sent them and I was mortified. They'd rejected them all as well, it was so far off from Winnie the Pooh and anything I would've ever chosen for any event much less my first and only baby shower. She and I both knew I would've been upset and they wanted the day to be full of joy. When I saw my husband after talking to Shannon, he gave me a big hug and kiss. He's horrible at keeping big things from me, especially since I always pick up on it and say something. That's the downside of being married to a Prophet – we don't miss anything! If you're acting funny, even for good reason, we'll feel it! After all that, things got exciting, I picked out every detail, got my cousin Sharles involved and they all made sure I rested while she handled the execution.

I thank God for her, my family and friends, the baby shower was absolutely beautiful and so much fun. We had lots of pictures and videos taken to document the memories, and I'm so glad we did because our dear friend Denise whom my husband and I call "Mama D" passed away shortly after.

We met her back in 2010 in business through her son Chris and she became like family to us over the years. She'd always text for holidays or just because to send us love, hugs, and keep us updated on her grand-babies. She was truly a gem, always positive and lit up every room she walked in, we miss her dearly and are grateful we got to share such a beautiful memory with her.

CHAPTER 6

The Gift and Hand of God

I wondered if our newest addition would come on my 43rd my birthday like his brother four years prior, but he waited eight more days for a new beginning. On August 7, 2024 at 8:07am I gave birth via c-section to our baby boy Nathan Akachi Wilkins-Agomo. Nathan means "Gift of God" and Akachi (Igbo – Nigerian) means "Hand of God". He was 7lbs 0oz and 18 inches long. When they called out his time of delivery the whole medical team was blown away. It was their first time delivering a baby where the date and time were the same. 8/7 at 8:07. Eight - new beginning. Seven - completion. A supernatural pregnancy indeed!

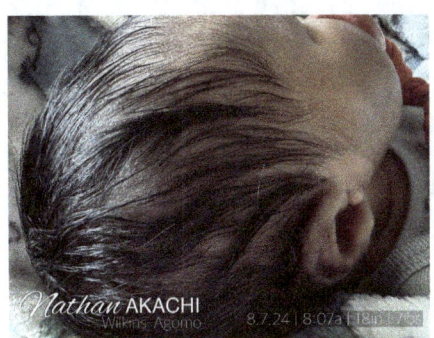

Aiden took his new promotion very seriously, wearing his big brother crown the hospital gave him, he made sure his baby brother's arrival got the attention deserved by pulling the code blue alarm in our hospital room. As the alarm filled our room, the entire hospital was alerted and every nurse on the floor ran to our room in sheer panic as emergency doctors prepared for their rescue mission. Meanwhile Daddy was asleep on the couch, without earplugs this time, Nathan was asleep in the crib as if he was wearing them instead and I was sitting on the bed in a diaper with swollen legs and feet the size of melons wondering what all the chaos was about. A quick scan of the room by one of the nurses let her know it was a mistake so she quickly turned it off. Aiden was standing in the corner with his hands held together and eyes wide and glossy ready to cry. I could tell from his look he was the culprit. I asked him did he touch a button, and he said yes, I'm sorry. I touched the blue one as the tears streamed down his cute little knew-he-wasn't-supposed-to-touch-anything face. He apologized to everyone through-out the day and leveraged his conversational charm to create a diversion and not get kicked out. I couldn't help but think of the commotion and shenanigans in store with the Aiden and Nathan royal brother duo. For Your glory Lord, we're buckled up and ready!

We were in the hospital for a couple of days before getting dis-charged. Everything was smooth, my pain was much lighter than my previous c-section even though it took longer to complete because of all the scar tissue. It made night feedings easier getting up and down out my rocker, recliner that I slept in for the first couple of months. It was more comfortable to sit up than lay down.

Nathan is really growing fast. Some days he looks like me, some days his Daddy, all cute and handsome as can be. He was holding his head up at two weeks old, and scooting on the floor trying to crawl at four weeks. Just the other day I saw him stomping his foot like the cartoon character he saw on his big brother's iPad. He is indeed developing supernaturally and Aiden is thrilled to have his new side kick. He's such an amazing big brother, Nathan locks in on everything he does, mustering up all the energy his tiny body can to try to join him, all just to crash on his side. We can image him thinking *"I'm coming big bro!"* Watching them grow up together is going to be such a blessing, I'm so grateful they have each other. When Apostle Boyd prophesied to me in 2019 that there would be *"noise in the house"* I had no idea the decibel to come! Things will be much louder with two boys and sleep will be rare for a while, and I'm grateful for it all.

You know what! I just realized as I'm typing this, it is November again. WOW! The Lord told me the other day to write and finish this book this month. I'm also planning the first Supernatural Pregnancy Summit since giving birth to Nathan in January. It will be in Houston; at the same church we saw the pink fetus. I initially had one scheduled for March 2024, but Houston had a tornado and lost power all over the city for weeks. The Lord already told me to rest when I found out I was pregnant, but I felt maybe I could get one more Supernatural Pregnancy Summit in before I got too far long, so He sent a tornado to shut me down. I'm grateful for the correction and redirection because no matter how strong in faith I am, I'm still a child to Him that needs to be checked. I repented, tucked in my tail, sat my pregnant presumptuous self-down and did nothing until I knew for sure He spoke it. His will – not mine.

The mysteries of our Father are unmatched. What a joy it is to experience the mind of Christ. In spite of my tremendous imperfections, He still saw fit to make me a sign and wonder of what building His Kingdom through your barrenness looks like. Apostle Boyd also prophesied that after the birth of my son Aiden *"there will be a supernatural birthing for women all over the world"*. It is so.

Will you yield your will to the Father so He can do the same for you? The reward is worth the weight of the wait.

CHAPTER 7

It's Brewing in Your Belly

Your promise. Your baby. Your spouse. Your business. The things you're believing God for are already brewing in your belly and in order for you to witness the full manifestation of them you must do the work. Execute your assignment. Along my journey I fasted, I prayed and I leaped. In-spite of not knowing what would happen, how it would happen, who would participate, where I'd do it or where I'd go, I executed. I fasted. I prayed. I leaped. While I was working, the promise He wanted to give me was brewing in my belly and I was further along in the process than I thought I could be.

I prophesy a time traveling anointing over your life! Time will fast forward to get your promise to you and you will supernaturally skip steps. There will be an exponential advancement and things that would normally take weeks will only take seconds. May a supernatural consolidation of time be upon you, in Jesus's name! Amen!

Glory to the Lord! Listen, the fact that I was unknowingly supernaturally pregnant while ministering about supernatural pregnancy is mind blowing to me. Think about what you're called to do and the miracles that await you within the build of it.

I decree and declare an excavation of assignments for you. Father, in the name of Jesus, dig up old projects that have been buried and dormant in their memory. Bring it to the forefront of their mind so they can see it clearly, dust off the delay and make it plain so they and others can read and run with it, in Jesus's name. Amen!

I wasn't even seeking the gift He gave, yet I am filled with so much joy and excitement because it's a testament to the Father's exceedingly abundantly above all.

> *Ephesians 3:20-21 NKJV - Now to Him who is able to do exceedingly abundantly above all that we ask or think, according to the power that works in us, to Him be glory in the church by Christ Jesus to all generations, forever and ever. Amen.*

He gave me what I didn't know to ask for because He knew I needed it. Now that we have Nathan I couldn't imagine our lives without him. Two sons – the heir and the spare as my husband says. After Aiden was born, I didn't think I had capacity for more love, it wasn't possible considering our testimony and the way my heart explodes with joy at the thought of him. But God increased my capacity. He did so through my building and believing for others. When any of the Supernatural Mamas in waiting tell me they're pregnant or share a medical miracle I cry tears of joy as if it is my own surprise. Just yesterday one of the ladies in our Supernatural Mamas group told me, after years of trying and countless setbacks, she is now five months pregnant. She wanted to wait until she was further along to share.

Another supernatural mama told me after thirteen years of waiting, she gave birth to twins at the beginning of the year! Many of these women are conceiving naturally, after trying IVF and other means that didn't work.

Another woman was told by her doctor she has no more eggs left, yet she still believes because the timing and things that are happening around her are so reminiscent of my story that she is excited about the negative report from her doctor. She is choosing to believe the report of the Lord and moving forward to finish building the assignment the Father gave her that she abandoned long ago. We celebrated her news, not only because we know her promise is close, but because she has chosen to build His Kingdom through her barrenness.

His thoughts of us and promises for us are so much greater than we can truly comprehend. According to the Merriam Webster dictionary there are roughly over one million words that exist in the English language alone, and based on our upbringing thousands more slogans. Even that is too small to describe what The Father thinks of us and wants to do for us.

> Isaiah 55:8 NKJV - "For My thoughts are not your thoughts, Nor are your ways My ways," says the Lord

As you build His Kingdom through your barrenness and hit a stumbling block, challenge or setback remember this; if it has a name - He is above it. He's even above Heaven itself. The Bible tells us He stretches out the heavens like a veil and spreads them out like a tent to dwell in. If He stretches a tent then he's bigger than it. A tent that covers all of heaven and earth can't hold him. Nothing can. There is power and confidence in knowing we serve a God so great, mighty and powerful, who created and controls everything, yet is still in the midst of all things, including our thoughts and feelings. You've heard and have probably said the phrase the devil is in the details, usually that's because something bad or unexpected happens. That's the wrong thing to prophesy over your life! The devil isn't omnipresent he isn't at all places and in all things, so the details for your life belong to the Lord. Your Helper – the Holy Spirit is who is in the details. What seems like a setback in the natural is a set up for the supernatural. He sees what we can't because He's omniscient, so the detour isn't a burden sent by the devil, but a redirection sent by the Lord. You just don't know it's a blessing until you keep working and get to the other side to complete your assignment.

> *Isaiah 40:22 AMP - It is He who sits above the circle of the earth, and its inhabitants are like grasshoppers; [It is He] who stretches out the heavens like a veil and spreads them out like a tent to dwell in.*

CHAPTER 8

Know Your Seasons

Another thing my experience has taught me is to honor the seasons. There are seasons of separation, preparation and elevation.

Ecclesiastes 3:1 NKJV - To everything there is a season, a time for every purpose under heaven. During the season of separation, you take that time to disconnect from the people, places and things that aren't serving you at that time. Doesn't mean they or it is always bad, they just aren't right or good for where you are so you love them/it alone until you're at a place where you can reengage and it not negatively impact anything you're doing. In some cases, you can cut off all communication, in others you may not be able to because those you need to separate from are family. In those cases, you limit interaction and information. Too many cooks in the kitchen creates chaos. Put up a healthy boundary and if needed let them know, you need to focus on a few things and you'll circle back to them when done. During this time your focus should be hearing solely from the Lord through prayer and fasting. The bible says in *Luke 5:16 "But Jesus Himself would often slip away to the wilderness and pray [in seclusion]."* Your separation provides a supernatural cleansing so you can re-calibrate and be prepared to build bigger and better, anyone who feels it is unnecessary or anything that is distracting all must be included in the separation.

Matthew 4:1-11 NKJV - Then Jesus was led up by the Spirit into the wilderness to be tempted by the devil. And when He had fasted forty days and forty nights, afterward He was hungry. Now when the tempter came to Him, he said, "If You are the Son of God, command that these stones become bread." But He answered and said, "It is written, 'Man shall not live by bread alone, but by every word that proceeds from the mouth of God.' " Then the devil took Him up into the holy city, set Him on the pinnacle of the temple, and said to Him, "If You are the Son of God, throw Yourself down. For it is written: 'He shall give His angels charge over you,' and, 'In their hands they shall bear you up, Lest you dash your foot against a stone.' " Jesus said to him, "It is written again, 'You shall not tempt the Lord your God.' " Again, the devil took Him up on an exceedingly high mountain, and showed Him all the kingdoms of the world and their glory. And he said to Him, "All these things I will give You if You will fall down and worship me." Then Jesus said to him, "Away with you, Satan! For it is written, 'You shall worship the Lord your God, and Him only you shall serve.' " Then the devil left Him, and behold, angels came and ministered to Him.

This isn't a time to explain yourself, partly because it's a discovery process that you don't fully understand yourself. You just know in order for things to change, things must change, and as you walk out one change you discover the next one. Once you've taken your time to get settled in the Lord, and are clear on what He wants you to do next, then you enter into the next season.

During the season of preparation is where you take time to get clarity on your vision and *"make it plain"* per Habakkuk 2:2 and the potential sacrifice it will require. While there's no way to know all the costs up front, the clear mindset from your season of separation period will have equipped you to sift and sort accordingly. The bible says in *Luke 14:28 AMP - For which one of you, when he wants to build a watchtower [for his guards], does not first sit down and calculate the cost, to see if he has enough to finish it?* Beginning is great, you don't want to be idle but the goal is to finish and in order to do that you must prepare. Take inventory of your life, your finances, friendships, family, connections etc... in order to advance in any of those areas, you must know what you're working with so you can, plan properly and build from there. If you want to make a big purchase like a car or house you must count the costs first to see how much you can afford. Your eyes may say Bentley but the budget may say Buick. Both are great cars that will take you from point A to point B but they are vastly different in their costs and what's required of you to purchase. You may be able to buy a $500,000 home, but that doesn't mean you can afford it. The same applies with your purpose work, you may have the vision to do something massive, but can you execute it properly or will it end up half done because you weren't prepared for it? You want a baby, great! Are you mentally, emotionally, financially and spiritually prepared to handle the unexpected costs with trying to get pregnant then raising the child? Are you willing to tarry and faint not until it comes to pass? *Galatians 6:9 AMP - Let us not grow weary or become discouraged in doing good, for at the proper time we will reap, if we do not give in.* We don't know what we don't know so it's important to do all that you can in the natural with proper expectation knowing you prepared so when the supernatural shows up you can maintain and honor what you received. Remember the goal isn't to just start, it's to finish.

Once you've done the work to become the person, you're ready for your season of elevation. You have what you wanted, you've accomplished the goal you set, you're pregnant finally, or delivered your baby, your business is growing, you're engaged or married, all cylinders are going and you're winning. This is a great time that comes with its own set of circumstances. The people you separated from may want to come back around or they may not and if you did the work on yourself properly, you're OK either way. Maintaining the promise is your priority, and for that you need the right people in the right places in your life. More on that later.

Each season requires its own sacrifice and execution strategy. Your off-season practice prepares you for your in-season play. Proper response to all seasons is critical to your ability to execute properly. The communication from heaven is different during each time. When I attempt to do something out of season it doesn't work. There is a time to launch and a time to prepare for the launch. There is a learning season and a testing season. When you're in learning mode, you're listening to the Lord. When you're in testing mode you're applying what He told you. Taking the test requires your full participation and focus. While you wait for the results there are many feelings and questions you have. Am I prepared for the result? What if I fail? What do I do afterwards?

With each season you experience; you learn more about what to do and what not to do. You're more confident in your ability because you're closer to the One who gave you the power and ability to create in the first place. A person can be talked out of what they think and even what they believe, but very rarely can you talk someone out of what they know. We know what we experience because we lived it. Once you experience the Lord carrying and keeping you, restoring and leading you, forgiving and healing you, there is no doubt that He is real. It's those experiences that lay the foundation to the radical faith that you will need and use along your journey of building His Kingdom through your barrenness.

CHAPTER 9

Identify Your Resources

Who is in your corner? Covering and accountability are critical. Whether you're a part of a church or ministry or not it's important to have someone that you can go to for wisdom and correction. People you respect enough to listen to.

> *Proverbs 15:22 AMP - Without consultation and wise advice, plans are frustrated, but with many counselors they are established and succeed.*

Mentorship isn't just for business, it's for life and ministry as well. Some call them spiritual father or mother, based on their relationship, but regardless of the title you give them their purpose is to help guide you. People are resources; their time, talent, and treasure are all tools that can help you execute your assignments. Some mentor closely, some mentor from a far. Mentors have gone deeper into the waters of life and can provide wisdom without you getting the same wounds they did along their journey. Identify who your helpers are and use discernment when assigning them a role in your life. Understand there will be disappointments along the way because you're dealing with people and we all have our flaws. Even Jesus couldn't escape it from the twelve disciples - Peter denied Him three times (Matthew 26:69-75) and Judas betrayed him (John 13:21-27, Mark 14:43-50, Matthew 26:48-54 and

Matthew 27:3). Familiarity breeds contentment. The closer you are the more common you become. To avoid this, keep a healthy boundary.

There are three categories of people you will need in your life. Those who are where you were will remind you of your growth and give you an opportunity to pour back. Those who are where you are, will serve as an accountability partner and neutral support system. Those who are where you want to be are who you call when you need to be by the fire. They make your baby leap the most, fuel you and serve as a reference point for what's possible.

Above all, God is the ultimate source, no one and nothing is above Him. Don't make your mentor your master and don't make your desire your idol. It's ok to want your promise badly, but never more than you want to the Lord. When you prioritize Him as the source, He will make sure you will never run out of resources. Praising the Lord isn't contingent on what He does for you. Whether you get what you want or not, He is still God. He is still faithful. He still loves you and will always provide. Full stop!

CHAPTER 10

You Must Participate in
Your Own Rescue

The Father wants to bless you, and He will but you have to do your part. Many of His blessings are unexpected – a supernatural surprise – getting pregnant with Nathan, is an example of that for me, but a lot of what He wants to do for us is conditional. Condition means: To have a significant influence on or determine (the manner or outcome of something). Something that must exist in order for something else to happen. Conditions are the checks and balances of our faith. Your conditions determine the outcome, they don't determine the journey. They also cause you to weigh your decisions. It's an IF/THEN dance. If you do A then you get B. **If** - introduces the condition. **Then** - introduces the promise.

*1 Kings 6:11-12 NKJV - Then the word of the Lord came to Solomon, saying: "Concerning this temple which you are building, **if** you walk in My statutes, execute My judgments, keep all My commandments, and walk in them, **then** I will perform My word with you, which I spoke to your father David.*

*Matthew 6:14-15 AMP - For **if** you forgive others their trespasses [their reckless and willful sins], (**then**) your heavenly Father will also forgive you. But **if** you do not forgive others [nurturing your hurt and anger* *with the result that it interferes with your relationship with God], **then** your Father will not forgive your trespasses.*

*Exodus 19:5 AMP - Now therefore, **if** you will in fact obey My voice and keep My covenant (agreement), **then** you shall be My own special possession and treasure from among all peoples [of the world], for all the earth is Mine;*

*2 Chronicles 7:14 NKJV - **if** My people who are called by My name will humble themselves, and pray and seek My face, and turn from their wicked ways, **then** I will hear from heaven, and will forgive their sin and heal their land.*

*Matthew 17:20 AMP - He answered, "Because of your little faith [your lack of trust and confidence in the power of God]; for I assure you and most solemnly say to you, **if** you have [living] faith the size of a mustard seed, you will say to this mountain, 'Move from here to there,' and **(then)** [if it is God's will] it will move; and nothing will be impossible for you.*

There are more scriptures to support this but I want to pause here and highlight the *[if it is God's will]* part of the scripture above because it makes it so plain. **IF** the condition you execute for your promise aligns with His will, **THEN** He will bless you. Nothing outside of His will for you will work in the end. Wrong can look right for a while, but the fruit of it will eventually show it wasn't the Lord's doing. When your flesh is involved, it can be hard to tell. Deception is the main tool in the devil's toolbox, he is the father of lies and will try anything he can to make you think you're heading in the right direction, only to lead you to death and destruction. Think about when he convinced Eve to eat the apple God told them not to touch. An apple as it is isn't bad, one a day keeps the doctor away, right? Yes, unless the Lord tells you not to eat it! Then that same nutritious apple becomes poison keeping your blessing away!

All success isn't from the Lord just as all growth isn't progressive. Discernment is key!

Sometimes the conditions are completely unrelated to the promise. The promise may be a baby, but the condition is relocating like He told you to. The promise may be a husband, but the condition is applying for a new job. You wouldn't think one had anything to do with other, but knowing that His thoughts are not ours we can't count it out we just need to obey. The condition could also be directly related to the promise. Go apologize to your Husband, and make love to him. Yes, he was wrong and upset you, but this is ovulation week and its prime baby making time! Yes, you're going through IVF. No, you don't have fallopian tubes - so what! You're ripe for a miracle, now go to your appointment to participate in your own rescue! If you read my first book, *You're Not Infertile. You're Just Not in Timing* you'll know I'm a witness of the importance of keeping your appointments. It was at an appointment that I didn't set, but the doctor had on their books for me, that I discovered my fibroid removal miracle. After having surgery in 2014 to remove eight, two of them came back two years later. I prayed for the Lord to remove them and He did! I didn't set that appointment, but the doctor called me to tell me I had one, I knew God was up to something so I went. A supernaturally set appointment had the miracle I'd been praying for and a message I couldn't ignore. It was critical to my testimony! There is always something on the other side of your obedience. It can be the promise or another test, we don't know until we participate.

Prophetic Release: The Lord wants to make a concession for you. A concession is a preferential allowance. He is breaking systems, structures and rules just for you. The Father says stay in position, focused on His mission for your life because your concession is coming.

It's in the build that you discover the baby. A lot of people like to wait until there is fruit then start to produce, when it is your production that leads to the fruit. You have to start building first and as you build, you'll discover more about what you're birthing. Remember the season of separation I talked about earlier? You have to complete every step. You're not going to get the full playbook upfront, that's just not how it goes. You'll see the goal and maybe steps along the way but the full picture of the promise is revealed during the build. The playbook itself is concealed in the heart of the Father and those of us who are on the other side of some of our battles can agree, had the Lord showed us the playbook upfront of what's to come we more than likely would've opted out of even pursuing it.

CHAPTER 11

Calling vs Assignment

A calling is predetermined and for life. It's what you were set a part to do in Jeremiah 1:5 before you were formed in your mother's womb. A calling will chase you. Correct you. Confirm you. Cleanse you. It will also consolidate you. Consolidate means to make something physically stronger or more solid. To be combined into a more coherent whole. Coherent means logical and consistent. You are stronger, more solid and coherent when you are doing what you are called to do.

An assignment is a task that you must execute to complete your calling. Assignments are frequent and used to keep you on track. They are the boxes you must check on the callings to-do list.

Jesus's calling was to sacrifice His life for our sins. His assignments were the miracles He performed and teaching He did along the way. When you no longer want to execute an assignment, your calling is what course corrects you, putting you back on track.

> *Philippians 3:13-14 AMP - Brothers and sisters, I do not consider that I have made it my own yet; but one thing I do: forgetting what lies behind and reaching forward to what lies ahead, I press on toward the goal to win the [heavenly] prize of the upward call of God in Christ Jesus.*

The thing that lies behind, as Apostle Paul states are his assignments – the ones he passed and the ones he failed, one thing is for sure you don't always get it right along the way and you can't sit and celebrate what you got right forever. The call is too great to just sit. You must press on and build His Kingdom through your barrenness so He can bless you.

My calling as a Purpose Midwife is to show people by example how to activate their faith to give birth to their purpose, which is all the things God has called them to do. Every video, phone call, sermon, event, zoom meeting, conversation and the like, is an assignment along the way. Some more labor intensive than others, but all assignments nonetheless and all equally important to my calling. On November 2, 2024 I received another prophetic word from Dr. Yves Abraham, she is a licensed marriage and family therapist whose ministry focuses on blending clinical practices with biblical through her Kingdom Mental Health summits and programs. It was during another event hosted by Apostle Andrea Haynes where Apostle David Boyd whose prophesy to me in 2019 regarding the birth of Aiden came to pass, was also in attendance.

Dr. Yves prophesied:

"God is increasing your anointing, your grace, when it comes to the birthing. There is a multiplicity of grace that has been added onto you when you had that second child. That second child is not, I'm going to use normal for lack of a better word. That second child is not only a child of covenant but a child of establishment. God says, because you chose to honor Him and not be ashamed of the whole process, He says, I don't add when it comes to you, I multiply. You have not seen anything yet. It's going to get so big and so quick that people are going to be at your settings, and they're going to desire to have a baby and, in that moment, it's going to happen. God is going to erect sperm that had been laying dormant. They're going to think that they need to go sleep with their partner, but they won't need to because all God is going to do is erect, revive the sperm that is already in that female and they are going to

*leave the place pregnant. That's what God has imparted onto
you as reason of your obedience."*

I shared the video of this on social media and my website. As you
watch you can see the progression of my weeping as she's speaking.
What she and no one else knew was that I have dreams written in
my journal where the Lord has shown me exactly what He confirmed
through her. He has shown me women who walked into the Supernatural Pregnancy Summit barren and leave with successful implantation.
Women who came barren leave with pregnant bellies noticeable by all
with kicks she could feel. Women who came pregnant with babies that
had been pronounced deceased by her doctor, leave with that same baby
not only revived but birthed and in her arms. He's even gone as far as to
give the some of the names of these children, and they are bible era war-
riors for Christ!

I thought my dream was wild until I heard a testimony at a different
conference I attended in July 2023 at my church called the Mantle of
Deborah, hosted by Apostle Isi Igenegba from Nigeria. I'd never heard
of her or her ministry before, but was absolutely blown away when she
began to share her supernatural pregnancy testimony. It mirrored mine
through substance and timeline. She too was believing for a baby and
went through a transition in her ministry that was revealed once she executed the assignment the Father gave her. Out of her obedience and
birthing of her son came her conference that I was now sitting in. I was
in awe of the Father being so detailed and consistent. The fact that He
was doing the same thing for the both of us at the same time on different continents, then set it up for us to cross paths a few years later
where I'd receive revelation that not only made my baby leap but deliver!
One of the ministers who spoke was Dr. Patricia King. She shared a testimony from her friend Miranda Nelson, both whom I'd never met or
heard of before. During crusade in Africa a pregnant woman attended
looking for a miracle because her baby had been pronounced deceased
in her womb. She was desperate for a miracle and God delivered - her

baby came back alive right there at the crusade! I nearly passed out when I heard her say that. Matter of fact she was prophesying that to another minister in attendance. Not knowing it was also for me because a few weeks prior I had that same dream, wondering how on earth that would ever happen, because I'd never heard of it happening before. I needed faith to believe, so God used someone I didn't know, who wasn't even talking to me, share what He knew I needed to hear, so that I could have evidence of what He wants to do through me. The complexity of the mind Christ is unmatched. How blessed are we to even be able to communicate with Him. There was a commercial that came out years ago that called the actor the most interesting man in the world, I laugh because there's no one who can spark your interest fire like Jesus! A testimony like that during a time when I was in my season of preparation was truly a God send. He raises people from the dead all the time, but there was something about a deceased baby in the womb being brought back alive while still in the womb that amplified my faith. It's radical, yet I believe! The details surrounding when, how and where are up to the Father, being obedient to my calling is up to me. Have your way, Lord!

CHAPTER 12

The Weight of the Call

The responsibility of our calling creates a natural heaviness that causes hesitancy. Nothing in the natural says it is possible to do, so there's a hesitancy to begin. Happens to us all. Our faith in and fear of the Lord should be enough to get us over that emotional hump, and in most cases, it is, but many who have been consumed by the flesh add unnecessary weight to the wait. Disobedience, delay, distractions, delusions are all flesh related reactions to the unknown that make the calling heavier.

You don't feel the weight of the call until you start to walk in it, prior to that you only have an idea of it. Sitting with a 5-pound baby or barbell in your lap is one thing. Walking around with it in your hand or arms for an extended period of time is another! That cute little 5-pound angel quickly begins to feel like a 500-pound adult. This is why and where majority of people quit or self-sabotage by either sitting on their gifts and talents doing nothing or trying to carry too much too soon or fast.

Your calling is progressive, that's why assignments are necessary. Each assignment increases your strength. For example, you risk injury if you start your new workout plan trying to bench press 200 pounds day one. Wisdom says work your way up to it. I saw a viral video online of a super skinny guy in the gym decked out in name brand workout gear. He didn't have an ounce of muscles in his arms, but he looked like he was going to crush it, so I'm thinking this is about to be an epic transformation video! Instead of the transformation, the next scene in the video shows him at the same small size, holding two huge barbells. It was obvious they were too heavy for him, he could barely stand up! Then he looked in the mirror and did the teeniest, tiniest bicep curl. His arm barely moved a centimeter! He did those tiny moves super-fast, never actually making one full rep. His form was tragic, his face was red and legs trembling. He looked like he was about to pass out! He was right to be in the gym, but those weights were not a part of his assignment that day. Could he get there? Absolutely, but he needed to honor the 5, 10 and 15-pound weight assignments first.

That's how we look in the spirit attempting to short cut the process by skipping or half completing assignments. All we're doing is delaying the promise. The goal is to actually be strong in faith, not pretending while secretly living in fear. We don't attract what we pretend to be we attract what we are. Assignments are home base for the development of your character, so when the blessing comes you can maintain it! The bible says in Proverbs 18:16 - *your gifts make room for you and put you before great men*, which is amazing, but your gift can put you in a room that your character will get your kicked out of if you don't execute your assignments.

The more assignments we do the more grace we get, which means the more we can carry because grace growth is exponential. Peter and John's journey in Acts chapter one through chapter four is a great example of that. With each assignment they executed came an amplification of the glory of the Lord. They were able to perform many miracles, stand firm in the face of adversity and persecution and bring thousands of souls to Christ. In Acts chapter one they received impartation at the Upper Room. In chapter two, Pentecost, Peter preached his first sermon saving 3,000 souls. In chapter three there was demonstration of healing so powerful that everyone began to pay attention. Peter preached his second sermon saving 5,000 souls. In chapter four they reached a new level of the glory of the Lord, so much so their presence alone was enough to perform miracles. That brought upon imprisonment and being told the name of Jesus was forbidden to use. Yet they continued which shifted the atmosphere and ultimately their vindication.

Everyone has a calling; therefore, everyone has an assignment. Mary's calling was to carry and birth the Messiah – Jesus. One of her assignments along the way was to go see her cousin Elizabeth.

> *Luke 1:39-45 AMP - Now at this time Mary arose and hurried to the hill country, to a city of Judah (Judea), and she entered the house of Zacharias and greeted Elizabeth. When Elizabeth heard Mary's greeting, her baby leaped in her womb; and Elizabeth was filled with the Holy Spirit and empowered by Him. And she exclaimed loudly, "Blessed [worthy to be praised] are you among women, and blessed is the fruit of your womb! And how has it happened to me, that the mother of my Lord would come to me? For behold, when the sound of your greeting reached my ears, the baby in my womb leaped for joy. And blessed [spiritually fortunate and favored by God] is she who believed and confidently trusted that there would be a fulfillment of the things that were spoken to her [by the angel sent] from the Lord."*

On the other side of Mary's obedience to her assignment of going to see Elizabeth was a sign and wonder – her baby leaped! Here's why that was so significant – unbeknownst to Elizabeth and Mary, Elizabeth was pregnant with John the Baptist whose calling was to prepare the way for Jesus.

John the Baptist's calling was connected to Mary's assignment. He received impartation and activation. The moment John the Baptist and Jesus's mothers did their part they were given power and confirmation to do theirs. The recognition of that is what caused John the Baptist to leap in the womb! The leap was activation. In that moment the supernatural clock started counting down to the ultimate testimony of Jesus our Messiah! Assignments bring Activation which brings Equipment.

You become a magnet for the supernatural! All the resources show up! Sometimes at your door!

That's why building His Kingdom through your barrenness is so important – what and who you're purposed to give birth to isn't normal, common or light. It's massive, world changing, inspiring and nation saving! I know it's heavy right now and things feel really tough but you must press on. Before you doubt and count yourself out of qualification remember this.

God wants to do the un-ordinary through you. He wants to break protocol for you! All you have to do is surrender to Him. Despite setbacks, setups, doubters, naysayers and the like you must know that on the other side of your assignment is a sign and wonder that no one will be able to deny or ignore.

> *Acts 4:13 AMP - Now when the men of the Sanhedrin (Jewish High Court) saw the confidence and boldness of Peter and John, and grasped the fact that they were uneducated and untrained [ordinary] men, they were astounded, and began to recognize that they had been with Jesus. And seeing the man who had been healed standing there with them, they had nothing to say in reply.*

"And seeing you" at your wedding after being told you'll never be a wife – *they will have nothing to say.*

"And seeing you" with your family celebrating the arrival of your new baby after years of waiting – *they will have nothing to say.*

"And seeing you" decorate your dream home after bankruptcy – *they will have nothing to say.*

"And seeing you" driving your new car after repossession – *they will have nothing to say.*

"And seeing you" walk across the stage graduating summa cum laude (with the highest praise and honors) with your PhD after dropping out of high-school – *they will have nothing to say.*

"And seeing you" with your promise, whatever it may be – *they will have nothing to say.*

Whether you're barren in your fertility, finances, friendships, family, career, ministry, health or any challenge, when you build His Kingdom through your barrenness and He blesses you, they will have nothing to say - *because they will recognize you had been with Jesus.*

Take what you have and build it big. When life gives you more, take that and build some more. Your barrenness is connected to your build. God will put you under what He's called you to be over. You're only under barrenness because you're already predestined to be over it! It's under your feet, all you have to do is keep walking. You're on the winning team and victory is yours! All you have to do is build His Kingdom through it and He will bless you.

PorsheaWilkins

PURPOSE MIDWIFE.
AUTHOR. ENTREPRENEUR.

Porshea Wilkins-Agomo (born Porshea Mitchell of Hearne, Texas) is a Purpose Midwife, Author and Entrepreneur who resides in Houston, Texas with her Husband Jarrod, and their children.

PURPOSE MIDWIFE
In 2014, while recovering from a myomectomy to remove multiple grapefruit size fibroids from her uterus, God gave her the assignment for her Supernatural Pregnancy ministry where she serves as a Purpose Midwife for thousands of women globally. She uses biblical strategies to teach those assigned to her how to push past their pain and give birth to their purpose. Porshea is also the Founder of the Supernatural Pregnancy Summit, an event catered to women and couples battling infertility.

AUTHOR
Her first book, *You're Not Infertile, You're Just Not in Timing* - supernatural strategies to activate your faith in fertility - showcases her uncommon faith activating journey to conceive her miracle baby boy. Serving as evidence to all that when you practice God's principles you can participate in His promises. Her second book *Build My Kingdom Through Your Barrenness and I Will Bless You*, details the double portion supernatural pregnancy surprise the Lord gave her as she was tarrying on the front line for others who were believing for children.

ENTREPRENEUR
Porshea is Founder of the Virtual Business Boutique; a branding, marketing and web design agency. She also leads an organization of professionals across multiple continents in the Network Marketing profession alongside her Husband. Their vision to Build It For Your Last Name (BIFYLN) has allowed them to develop one of the most admired organizations in the profession.

EDUCATION + ACCOLADES
Porshea earned a B.B.A. in Marketing from Sam Houston State University in Huntsville, Texas, received Congressional Recognition for community development and managed the development of a $1.4 Billion brand in the retail industry.

CONNECT ON SOCIAL MEDIA

 @PorsheaWilkins

ACROSS ALL PLATFORMS

FOR BOOKING & MEDIA:
PorsheaWilkins.com

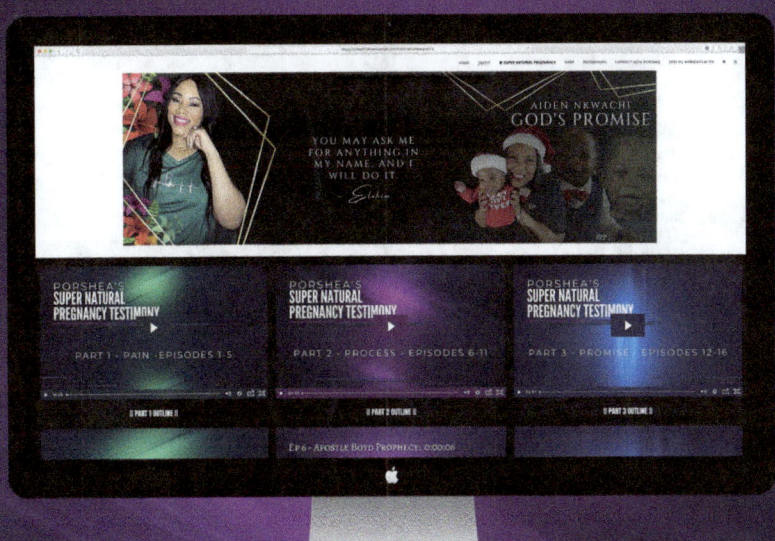

PORSHEA'S
SUPER NATURAL PREGNANCY DOCUSERIES
Reviews

 Pinky Brenda Matsie
5h · 🌐

Yooooo the way I am crying watching this. If you don't believe God can do it for you, I AM TELLING YOU RIGHT NOW HE CAN. Please please please please watch this. This should be on Netflix. Please go to this side and watch all episodes. Porshea Wilkins-Agomo 😭😭😭😭 😭😭😭😭😭😭 yooo.

 Renee Holmes
I watch it and this came at a time where I have been having issues with infertility I know God is in control no matter what

Love · Reply · 8h · Edited   ❤️ 1

I was on a walk when I listened to the docuseries and when I tell you this caught me completely off guard. I walked three miles, couldn't stop walking till I finished! I was at first like, who told her I had been trying to get pregnant?! Then the tears came...your testimony and the testimonies of the other ladies were so powerful! The power touched me through the screen!! It is always so refreshing to see the evidence of God's glory! This gave such a positive charge to my faith! Thank you for including me and thinking of me! ❤️ 😊

I am listening to your series and it's a nail biter!!!! This is so awesome and so great to hear. I'm 1/2 way through part 2 and so excited to hear the rest. We are currently out in California working towards IVF. And the amount of prophetic words and dreams are just amazing. But i feel so encouraged by how you pressed in with prayer. I need to post up and step my game up 😊💗💗🕯️🔥🔥Thank you for sharing your awesome testimony!

 natalieshavon Thank you for sharing your testimony. As a stage 4 endometriosis survivor, I sometimes get triggered by fertility stories, yet am still believing God for my spouse and for our conceived children. I just avoided reading an article about a celebrity with past fertility struggles, only to come across this video. I'm glad I watched till the end. It's a much needed reminder that God is still in the miracle business.

17h 1 like Reply

 Nnamdi Jarrod Wilkins-Agomo is with **Porshea Wilkins-Agomo**.
⭐ Favorites · September 15 at 11:18 AM · 🌐

🐑 LADIES LISTEN TO THIS TESTIMONY 🐑

There can be no Testimony without a Test and you will never get promoted to the next level until you pass the test.

I didn't know that giving birth to a child would require so much Faith, trust, consistency and commitment. I didn't know how many Women struggle with getting pregnant especially Kingdom Women until my wife Porshea Wilkins & I couldn't for almost 6 years.

If you've been struggling with Infertility in any area of your life weather it's getting pregnant to give birth to a Child, Business, Marriage or any other area of your life, please watch this video series now!!

Porshea Wilkins-Agomo lays out exactly step by step everything she did in the natural that put pressure on the Word of almighty Jehovah God to pour out a Supernatural blessing in the form of our baby boy Aiden.

Faith comes by hearing and hearing by the Word of God. 🐑

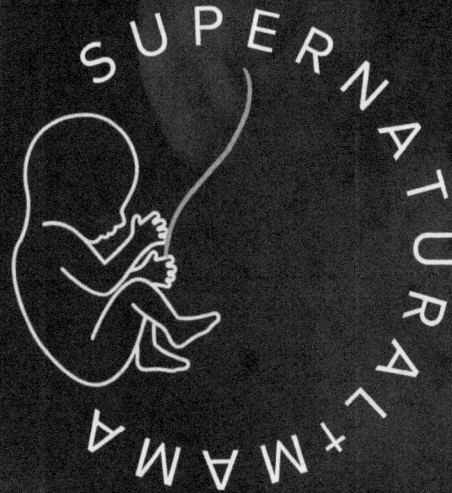

SUPERNATURAL†MAMA

It doesn't just take a village to raise a child, it takes a village to create one as well. Your village of support is here and ready to serve you.

register to join us monthly for prayer, counsel and more.
SupernaturalPregnancy.com

Available on iTUNES and
MidwifeMoments.com

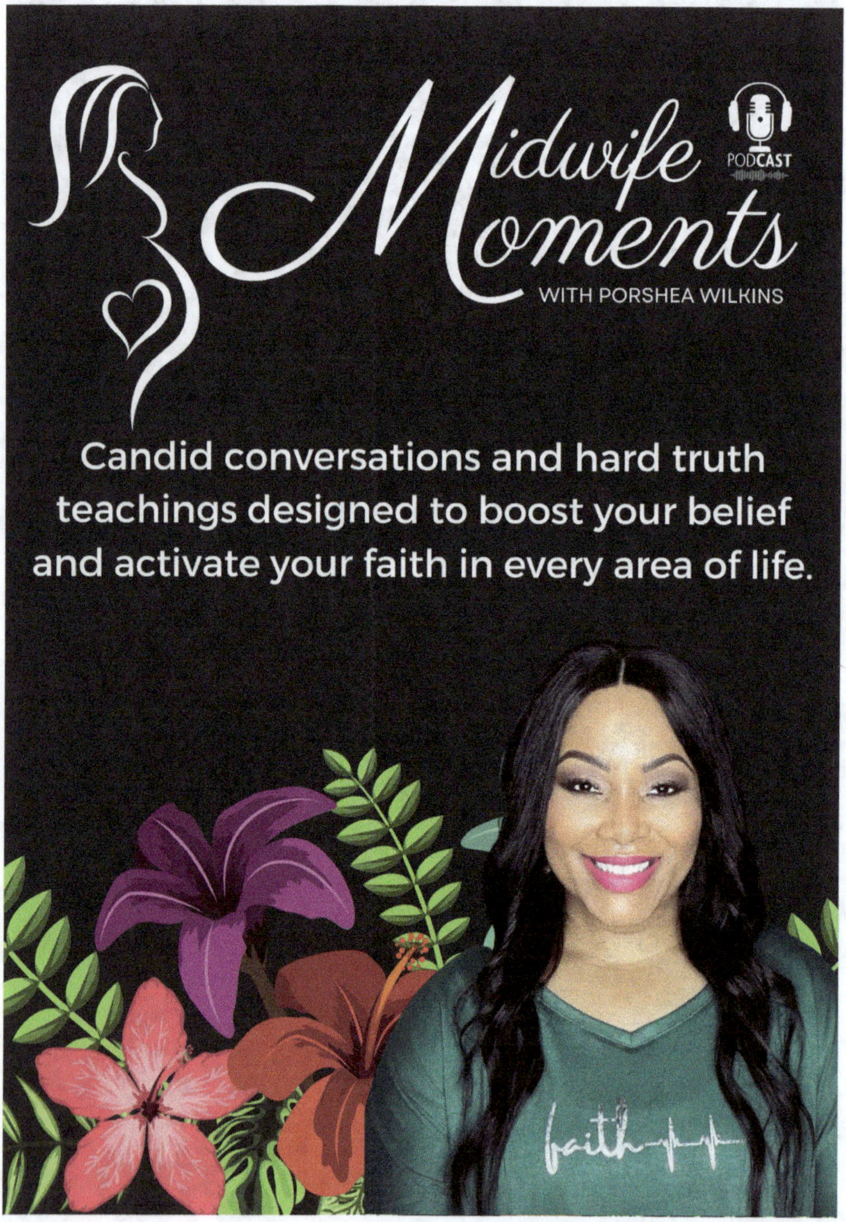
Midwife Moments
PODCAST
WITH PORSHEA WILKINS
Candid conversations and hard truth teachings designed to boost your belief and activate your faith in every area of life.
faith

www.ingramcontent.com/pod-product-compliance
Lightning Source LLC
Chambersburg PA
CBHW071543120626
46550CB00006B/2561